Book One

Mary 23 (room) (nos)

The Chester Books of

CELEBRATED SONGS

Selected and edited by
SHIRLEY LEAH

CONTENTS

CHESTER MUSIC

(A division of Music Sales Limited)
8/9 Frith Street, London W1V 5TZ

PREFACE

The Chester Books of Celebrated Songs are a graded series of volumes designed to provide a growing repertoire of fine songs in a progression related to their musical and technical difficulty and their suitability for the student singer. The books include music from the sixteenth to the twentieth centuries along with some folk song arrangements, most of which may be sung by either male or female voice. French, German, Italian and Spanish texts underlay the vocal line as appropriate, and English translations are provided, where necessary, as a guide to the content of the songs rather than as alternative performing versions.

Brief notes indicate the principal technical and interpretative features of each song for the guidance of teachers and pupils using the collections as part of a progressive vocal course. The difficulty of the piano accompaniments has also been borne in mind when selecting material for these volumes, and most of the chosen songs have only moderately difficult piano parts, so that they may easily be tackled by singers working with pianists of limited experience and by teachers who act as their own accompanists.

Although primarily designed for the young singer, these books should appeal to all singers who do not already possess the individual songs, for above all, the aim has been to present a well balanced collection of some of the most beautiful vocal music of the last four hundred years which will be enjoyed by performers and audiences alike.

Cover picture: Wheatfield with lark *by Vincent van Gogh — by kind permission of the National Vincent van Gogh Museum, Amsterdam.*

STAR VICINO

Salvator Rosa

Italian
range

A good exercise in *cantabile* singing. Moderate tempo, very legato. A breath may be taken in bar 19, but only when practising.

HAVE YOU SEEN BUT A WHITE LILY GROW?

Anon

English
range

This very beautiful lute song dates from the first half of the 17th century. The ascending scale at the end of the opening phrase should be sung lightly and without crescendo. Beware of the words *toucht* and *smutcht* — the 'u' should be as in *hum*.

SILENT WORSHIP

George Frederick Handel

English
range

When singing the words *lily* in bar 12, and *lady* in bars 6 and 19, make sure you stress the first syllable and not the second. Aim at singing the first two bars in one breath, breaking after *lady*, but not breathing.

WHAT THEN IS LOVE?

Philip Rosseter

English
range

Burn and *turn* are tricky words to sing — say the word *bird* and aim for the same sound. Make use of the percussive 'b' in the second verse: 'Beauty is but a blooming'.

O CAN YE SEW CUSHIONS?

Scottish Cradle Song

English
range

This lullaby must be sung gently. If you find it difficult to sing the top Fs in bars 11, 13, 38 & 40 softly, imagine a diminuendo through the bar.

JEUNES FILLETTES

Anon

French
range

This is a French *Bergerette* or Shepherd's Song. Nimble diction is required here, so keep the tongue forward, using the tip against the top teeth.

BOIS EPAIS

Jean Baptiste Lully

French   range

Breathing spaces are scarce in this song, so you must take deep breaths quickly and silently.

LIKE TO A LINDEN TREE AM I

Anton Dvorak

English   range

Take care with the words *shadow* and *staying* — different sounds in speech, but almost identical in singing. Note the demisemiquavers in bar 6.

IF IT'S EVER SPRING AGAIN

Christopher le Fleming

English   range

Many of the phrases rise at the end and need plenty of support. Breathe after *bees* in the last phrase.

UNDER THE GREENWOOD TREE

Thomas Arne

English   range

Words by Shakespeare. Keep the song moving and the tone light. Bars 36 - 40 are tricky - listen carefully to intonation and beware of the augmented fourth in bar 45.

AN DIE LAUTE

Franz Schubert

German   range

A simple little song, but with a sense of urgency — it must be kept moving. Be sure you sing a dotted quaver in bars 5 & 7, and C natural in bar 13 where the key changes.

NOD

C. Armstrong Gibbs

English   range

This is a setting of a Walter de la Mare poem. *Dolce e molto legato* — sweetly and very smoothly.

STAR VICINO

SALVATOR ROSA
(1615-1673)

Star vicino al bell' idol che s'ama,
È il più vago diletto d'amor!

Star lontan da collei che si brama
È d'amor il più nesto dolor.

To be near the loved one
Is a delight of love!

To be far from a loved one
Is grief and anguish.

È il più va - go di - let - to_ d'a - mor! _ È il più

va - - - - - - - go di - let - to di -

- let - to d'a - mor, il_ più_ va - go di - let - to d'a - mor!

Star lon - tan da co -

HAVE YOU SEEN BUT A WHITE LILY GROW?

Poem by
BEN JONSON

ANONYMOUS LUTE SONG
arr Michael Holloway

SILENT WORSHIP

Words by
ARTHUR SOMERVELL

GEORGE FREDERICK HANDEL
(1685-1759)

Did you not hear my la-dy Go down the ___ gar-den sing-ing?

15
Though I am no-thing to_ her, Though she must rare-ly look at me, And

17
though I could nev - er woo_ her, I love her till I die.

19
Sure - ly you heard my la - dy Go down the_ gar - den sing - ing,

Si - lenc-ing all the song-birds: And set - ting the al - leys ring - ing, But

sure - ly you see my la - dy Out in the gar - den there.

Riv' - ling the glitt'ring sunshine, With a glo - ry of gold - en hair.

WHAT THEN IS LOVE BUT MOURNING?

PHILIP ROSSETER
(1575-1623)
tr. Carl Shavitz

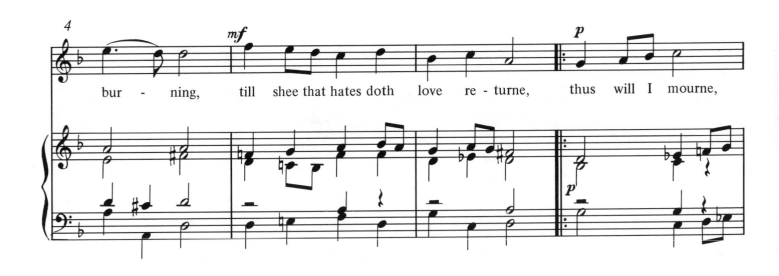

The bass line may be doubled by a viola da gamba or cello

What then is love but mourning?
   what desire but a selfe burning,
till shee that hates doth love return
thus will I mourne, thus will I sing
   come away, come away my darling.

Beautie is but a blooming,
   Youth in his glorie entombing;
Time hath a while which none can stay,
Then come away while thus I sing,
   Come away, come away my darling.

Summer in winter fadeth,
   Gloomie night heav'nly light shadeth,
Like to the morne are Venus flowers,
Such are her houres, then will I sing
   Come away, come away my darling.

(Thomas Campion)

Philip Rosseter
A Booke of Ayres 1601, part 2, XX

copy source: British Library

O CAN YE SEW CUSHIONS?

OLD SCOTTISH CRADLE SONG
arr. Michael Holloway

what will I do wi' you? Black's the life that I lead wi' you! Mo - ny o' you,

little__ for to gi'e you, Hee, O wee, O what will I do wi'__ you?

I've pla - ced my cra - dle on yon hol - ly

top, and aye as__ the__ wind blew, my__ cra - dle did rock. O

JEUNES FILLETTES

**EIGHTEENTH CENTURY
FRENCH BERGERETTE**
arr. Weckerlin

Jeune fillette, profitez du temps
La violette, se cueille au printemps,
La la la rirette, La ri lon lan la.

Cette fleurette passe en peu de temps
Toute amourette passe également
La la la rirette, La ri lon lan la.

Dans le bel age prenez un ami,
S'il est volage, rendez-le lui,
La la la rirette, La ri lon lan la.

*Young maiden, use the time
The violet to pick in the spring,
La la la rirette, La ri lon lan la.*

*The little flower dies after a short time,
And so does love.
La la la rirette, La ri lon lan la.*

*In your prime take a lover,
If he is fickle, pay him back.
La la la rirette, La ri lon lan la.*

Dans le bel â - ge Pre - nez un a - mi, S'il est vo -

la - ge, Ren - dez - le lui. Jeu - ne fil - let - te,

Pro - fi - tez du temps. La vi - o - let - te Se cueille au prin -

- temps._____ La la la ri - ret - te, La ri_ lon_ lan_ la,

la,_____ La la la ri - ret - te, La ri_ lon_ lan_ la.

BOIS EPAIS

from *Amadis*

JEAN BAPTISTE LULLY
(1632-1687)
arr Michael Holloway

Bois épais, redouble ton ombre,
Tu ne saurais être assez sombre,
Tu ne peux trop cacher mon malhereux amour.
Je sens un désespoir dont l'horreur est extrême,
Je ne dois plus voir ce que j'aime,
Je ne veux plus souffrir le jour.

Dense forest, thicken your shade,
You will never be too gloomy.
You cannot completely hide my unhappy love.
I feel a despair full of extreme anguish,
I am no longer allowed to see the one I love,
No more do I want to suffer daylight.

Andante con moto

jour. Je sens un dés - es - poir dont l'hor - reur est ex -

trê - me Je ne dois plus voir ce que j'ai - me,

Je ne veux plus souf - frir le jour.

colla voce

p a tempo

LIKE TO A LINDEN TREE

ANTON DVORAK
(1841-1904)

IF IT'S EVER SPRING AGAIN

Words by
THOMAS HARDY

CHRISTOPHER LE FLEMING
(b. 1908)

moor - cock splash'd, and hen

See - ing me

not, a - mid their floun - der,

Stand - ing

with my arm a - round her;

If it's

ev - er spring a - gain, Spring a - gain,

I shall

go where went I then.

If it's ev-er sum-mer time, Sum-mer time, With the

hay crop at the prime, And the cuc-koos two in

rhyme, As they used to be, or

UNDER THE GREENWOOD TREE

Words by
SHAKESPEARE

THOMAS ARNE
(1710-1778)

17 sweet bird's throat, And tune his mer-ry note Un-to the

21 sweet bird's throat, Come hi-ther, hi-ther, come

25 hither, come hither, come hi-ther, come hither, come hither, come hi-ther.

29

33 Here shall he see No en-e-my, But win-ter and rough wea-ther,

Here shall he see— No en-e-my, But win-ter and rough wea-ther,

Here shall he see— No en-e-my, But win - ter, but

win-ter and rough wea-ther.

Under the green-wood tree Who loves— to lie with

me,   And tune his mer - ry note   Un - to   the sweet bird's

throat,   And tune his mer - ry note   Un - to_ the sweet bird's

throat,   Come hi-ther,   hi-ther,   hi-ther,   hither,   come

hither, come hither, come hither, come hither, come hither, come hither, come hither.

AN DIE LAUTE

FRANZ SCHUBERT
(1797-1828)

Leiser, leiser, kleine Laute
flüstre was ich dir vertraute
dort zu jenem Fenster hin!
Wie die Wellen Sanfter Lüfte
Mondenglanz und Blumendüfte
Send es der Gebieterin.

Neidisch, sind des Nachbars Söhne
und in Fenster jener Schöne
flimmert noch ein einsam Licht
Drum noch leiser, kleine Laute
dich vernehme die Vertraute,
Nachbarn aber, Nachbarn nicht.

Softly, softly, little lute
Whisper what I said to you confidingly
There by the window!
On the gently lapping waves
Brilliant moonlight and scent of flowers
Send it to the mistress.

Envious are the neighbours' sons
and by the window of the pretty one
glimmers still one lonely light.
Play still softer, little lute,
Hear what I confide in you,
Let my loved one hear, but not the neighbours.

NOD

Words by
WALTER DE LA MARE

C. ARMSTRONG GIBBS
(1889-1960)

Printed and bound in Great Britain by
Caligraving Limited Thetford Norfolk

10/02 (45569)